RAILWAYS IN THE BRITISH LANDSCAPE

ROBIN COOMBES AND TALIESIN COOMBES

AMBERLEY

First published 2018

Amberley Publishing
The Hill, Stroud
Gloucestershire, GL5 4EP

www.amberley-books.com

ISBN 978 1 4456 8231 0 (print)
ISBN 978 1 4456 8232 7 (ebook)

British Library Cataloguing in Publication Data.
A catalogue record for this book is available from the British Library.

Origination by Amberley Publishing.
Printed in the UK.

INTRODUCTION

There is only one first time for anything. Writing this is special as it is the first introduction to our first book. It has long been an objective to produce a book, so thanks to all at Amberley Publishing for making it possible. Many of our photographs have appeared on social media and have been published in magazines, but there is something permanent about a book. The title, *Railways in the British Landscape*, is most appropriate as landscape is a major factor in determining the route a railway can follow and railways have had, over time, a massive impact on it.

First, a little bit of background – we are a father (Robin) and son (Taliesin) team that took up railway photography seriously in 2006. Although Robin has had a lifetime interest in all things related to railways, Taliesin comes with the fresh eyes of youth. We started with digital cameras so therefore have never used film, unlike past classic railway photographers.

We use Nikon equipment, simply because that was originally recommended but it has generally served us well. The photographs in the book have been taken with virtually the whole range of Nikon digital SLR cameras – a D80 to D5 – which, if nothing else, proves the type and resolution of the camera is important but not critical in capturing an image. Our aim has been to record railways, and in particular the steam locomotive in all its guises, in all winds and weather, from a distance or close up, in all different environments and including the people involved, so this selection of our photographs represents one small but important part of the total picture.

Two centuries ago the British landscape contained only a few canals, some indifferent turnpike roads and local unmade tracks plus a small number of mineral railways for transport. Although the steam engine had been invented for industry and early locomotives had run on rails, it was yet to make its mark. Over the next fifty years this was to change dramatically. Railways were laid to almost all towns throughout Britain, and because goods could be transported swiftly and easily by ever more powerful steam locomotives, cities were able to expand rapidly, with a range of industries.

The British landscape was changed forever. It is easy now to be unaware of railways in the landscape, hidden within cities in cuttings or behind buildings, and in the countryside lost in green tree-lined corridors. Often the odd bridge is the only clue to their existence. Equally, many trains are electric and almost silent, and apart from the occasional steam special or heritage line, the familiar trail of steam so characteristic of the past is no longer present to identify the speeding express or plodding goods train. Similarly, the hanging pall of smoke pointing to the location of the engine shed or railway station within towns has long gone.

It is hard to imagine a time when the building of a new railway was a modern marvel on a monumental scale with soaring viaducts, long, stark embankments and cuttings exposing the local geology. For the first time ordinary members of the public could travel deep underground in long tunnels at hitherto undreamt-of speeds of up to 60 mph. The railway stations, with their various styles of architecture, were often among the largest and grandest buildings in the town or city.

This book seeks to illustrate the variety of landscapes through which railways in Britain run: from the flat lands of East Anglia, through the rolling hills of middle England and the industrial cities and high fells of the North to the gorgeous coasts of the South West, the mountains of Wales and the remote Scottish moors. Each line had to be carefully surveyed because, as powerful as the steam locomotive was, to travel at speed with heavy loads railways needed to be laid with as few gradients and sharp curves as possible. Brunel's broad-gauge line from London to Bristol is a masterpiece of engineering with the gentlest of curves and gradients to allow fast running between the two cities, which can be contrasted with the equally difficult engineering challenge of the narrow gauge Ffestiniog Railway in Wales, which had to hug the mountain contours with sharp curves and steep gradients to bring slate from the quarries to the sea.

Rivers and estuaries also presented major obstacles but as a result we are blessed with some amazing bridges and viaducts – the Royal Albert crossing the Tamar, the Forth and Tay bridges being just three.

We hope that you will enjoy this collection. We planned to include something for everyone – from the railway enthusiast through to those who just enjoy the British landscape.

Robin and Taliesin Coombes
Cardiff
April 2018

Under the Pylons

BR 9F No. 92178 passes Swithland Sidings,
Great Central Railway, June 2015.

Cornish Viaduct

GWR Castle No. 5029 *Nunney Castle* and GWR King No. 6024 *King Edward I* cross Largin Viaduct, June 2010.

The Sea Wall

GWR Castle No. 5029 *Nunney Castle* heads the Cornishman through Dawlish, July 2011.

Under the Bridge

GWR Castle No. 5043 *Earl of Mount Edgcumbe*, Crofton, June 2011.

Dart Valley

GWR Pannier Tank No. 5786 runs along the River Dart at Hood Bridge, September 2010.

Snow Fields

GWR King No. 6024 *King Edward I* approaches Abergavenny, November 2010.

Along the Coast

GWR King No. 6024 *King Edward I* passing Dawlish, August 2011.

Leather on Willow

GWR Pannier Tank No. 9600 at Bledlow, July 2010.

Evening Glint

SR Battle of Britain No. 34067 *Tangmere*, Castle Cary, August 2011.

Taking the Shot

LMS Black 5s Nos 45407 and 44871 crossing Pinmore Viaduct, Pinmore, April 2010.

The Waverley

LMS Black 5s Nos 44871 and 45407 on the descent from Ais Gill, January 2012.

Station Lamps

Black 5 No. 44932 passes Gardsdale station, August 2011.

Summer on the S&C

Black 5 No. 45305 climbs to the summit at Ais Gill, July 2011.

Causeway

LMS Black 5s Nos 45407 and 44871 at Ardchronie, April 2011.

The Long Drag

LMS Royal Scot No. 46115 *Scots Guardsman* crossing the viaduct at Ais Gill, July 2011.

Midland Local

LMS 'Jinty' Tank No. 47406, Arley, Severn Valley Railway, March 2012.

Snow on the Hills

LMS 8F No. 48151 storms past Walsden, April 2012.

Sunset

LMS 8F No. 48624 on empty coals at Swithland, Great Central Railway, May 2016.

North Sea

LNER A4 No. 60007 *Sir Nigel Gresley* heads north at Berwick, April 2011.

Wind Swept

LNER A4 No. 60009 *Union of South Africa*
climbs to the summit at Ais Gill, February 2013.

The Tow Path

LNER A4 No. 60019 *Bittern* runs alongside the Grand Union Canal at Brinklow, March 2010.

Explosive Departure

LNER B1 No. 61264 departs Goathland, North Yorkshire
Moors Railway, November 2013.

Shafts of Steam, Sun and Steel

LNER K4 No. 61994, Rannoch Moor, October 2009.

Arches

BR Britannia No. 70013 *Oliver Cromwell* crossing Harringworth Viaduct, March 2011.

Welsh Marches Express

BR Britannia No. 70013 *Oliver Cromwell* at Pontrilas, November 2013.

A1 x A1

A1 Trust No. 60163 *Tornado* crosses the A1 Great North Road at Holloway, September 2009.

Terrace Housing

LNER A4 No. 60009 *Union of South Africa* crossing Durham Viaduct, Durham, May 2007.

Lamps

LNER A4s No. 60009 *Union of South Africa*, No. 60007 *Sir Nigel Gresley* and No. 60019 *Bittern* at Grosmont, North Yorkshire Moors Railway, April 2008.

Passing

BR Britannia No. 70013 *Oliver Cromwell* passes a Cross Country Class 220 Voyager at Bristol Temple Meads railway station, Bristol, June 2009.

Pink Dawn

LNER A4 No. 60009 *Union of South Africa* and LNER K4 No. 61994 *The Great Marquess* head south across Culloden Viaduct, Culloden, April 2007.

Morning Glint

LNER A4 No. 60009 *Union of South Africa* catches the
sun north of Wellingborough, December 2006.

Heading South

LNER A4 No. 60009 *Union of South Africa* and LNER K4 No. 61994 *The Great Marquess* head south across Findhorn Viaduct, Tomartin, April 2007.

Brunel Masterpiece

GWR King No. 6024 *King Edward I* and SR Battle of Britain No. 34067 *Tangmere* cross the Royal Albert Bridge, Saltash, August 2007.

Perfect Day

LMS Black 5 No. 45487 (aka No. 45407) crossing Loch Nan Uamh Viaduct, Àird Nam Bùth, October 2010.

Strath of Kildonan

LMS 8F No. 48151 crosses Craggie Water, Badfleugh, April 2007.

Wooded Valley

BR(WR) Manor No. 7827 *Lydham Manor* crosses Greenway Viaduct, Paignton & Dartmouth Railway, November 2014.

Journey's End

LMS 8F No. 48151 arrives at Thurso, having started at Penzance, April 2007.

Start of the Journey

GWR King No. 6024 *King Edward I* and GWR Castle No. 5051 *Earl Bathurst* depart Penzance for Thurso with the first Great Britain Railtour, April 2007.

Rainbow

GNR Y14 (J15) No. 564 (aka 65462) between Sheringham and Weybourne, North Norfolk Railway, November 2016.

Dart Estuary

BR (WR) Manor No. 7827 *Lydham Manor* crosses Greenway
Viaduct, Maypool, November 2014.

Silhouette

Countess of Warwick 0-6-0ST *Wissington* and a vintage train between Sheringham and Weybourne, March 2015.

Reflections at Victoria Bridge

GWR Manor No. 7812 *Earlstoke Manor*, Arley, Severn Valley Railway, March 2012.

Sun on the Moors

LMS Black 5 No. 44996 (aka 45407) passes Lochan a'Chlaidheimh, Rannoch Moor, October 2009.

West Coast Flyer

A Virgin Trains Class 390 Pendolino speeds past Little Haywood, April 2012.

Early Morning in the Suburbs

LMS Black 5 No. 45407 at Moses Gate, January 2015.

Railway Yards

GWR Castle No. 5043 *Earl of Mount Edgcumbe*, Washwood Heath, April 2017.

Suspended I

LNER A4 No. 60009 *Union of South Africa* crosses the Forth Bridge, August 2009.

The Roof of England

LNER A4 No. 60009 *Union of South Africa* crosses Ribblehead Viaduct, March 2013.

From the Beach

SR Battle of Britain No. 34067 *Tangmere* at Dawlish, September 2012.

Racing the Train

Beyer, Peacock & Co. Isle of Man No. 10 *G. H. Wood* races
a 1931 Swift Crusader at Scanton, Isle of Man, April 2014.

Cumbrian Mountain Express

LMS Princess Royal No. 6201 (aka 46201)
Princess Elizabeth at Waitby, August 2010.

Mixed Train

Fletcher, Jennings & Co. No. 1 *Tal-Y-Llyn* between Dolgoch
and Abergynolwyn, Talyllyn Railway, March 2015.

Saturday Morning Market

LNER A4 No. 60007 *Sir Nigel Gresley*, Chester-le-Street, September 2009.

Light on the Loch

LNER K1 No. 62034 (aka 62005) descends towards Corrour, October 2009.

Evening News

A diverted Virgin Trains Class 390 Pendolino passes
Bescot on a wet winter's evening, December 2007.

Waving

GNR Y14 (J15) No. 564 (65462) between Sheringham and Weybourne, North Norfolk Railway, November 2016.

Thunder over the City

Chiltern Railway DMU Class 168 No. 168214 waits at Birmingham Moor Street station, May 2009.

Evening Local

GWR Auto Tank No. 1450 and trailer, Toddington, Gloucester & Warwickshire
Railway, June 2017.

Regular Service

A1 Trust No. 60163 *Tornado* and DB Cargo Class 67 No. 67029 *Royal Diamond* crossing Ais Gill Viaduct with a Northern Rail Plandampf service, February 2017.

Autumn Steam

LMS Fairburn Tank No. 42073 passes the southern tip of Windermere, Lakeside & Haverthwaite Railway, November 2016.

LMS Black 5 No. 45305 passes Grisedale Common, February 2012.

A Difference of a Day I

S&D 7F No. 53808 descends Eardington Bank in sunshine, Eardington, Severn Valley Railway, March 2018.

A Difference of a Day II

S&D 7F No. 53808 descends Eardington Bank the following day in snow, Eardington, Severn Valley Railway, March 2018.

Looking after the Mighty

GWR *King Edward I* at Didcot Engine Shed, Didcot, May 2008.

Steam Age

SER O (O1) No. 65 (31065) makes ready for its duties.
Sheffield Park, Bluebell Railway, February 2007.

Signals

BR Britannia No. 70013 *Oliver Cromwell* departs Loughborough, Great Central Railway, November 2016.

Blue King

GWR King No. 6023 *King Edward II* climbs Eardington Bank,
Severn Valley Railway, March 2018.

Grazing

LSWR O2 No. 24 *Calbourne* at Ashey, Isle of White Steam Railway, March 2015.

The Jacobite

LMS Black 5 No. 45487 (aka 45407) departs Corpach, October 2010.

Border Crossing

Cross Country Class 220 Voyager crossing the Border Bridge between England and Scotland, Berwick-upon-Tweed, May 2012.

Eastern Line-Up

A1Trust No. 60163 *Tornado*, LNER A2 No. 60532 *Blue Peter* and LNER A4s Nos 60009 *Union of South Africa* and 60007 *Sir Nigel Gresley* at Barrowhill Roundhouse, Staverley, April 2009.

Northern Fells

LNER A3 No. 60103 *Flying Scotsman* crosses Lunds Viaduct, Moorcock, July 2017.

Shap Super Power

GWR Castle No. 5043 *Earl of Mount Edgcumbe* and LMS Duchess No. 46233 *Duchess of Sutherland*

Winter Wonderland

First Great Western BR Class 158 approaches Bradford on Avon, January 2013

Canal Reflections I

A1 Trust No. 60163 *Tornado* crossing Sands Viaduct,
Kidderminster, Severn Valley Railway, March 2018.

Sunburst

A Northern BR Class 158 leaves Ribblehead railway station, Ribblehead, January 2016.

Roaring over the Viaduct

LMS Black 5 No. 45212 and LNER K1 No. 62005 cross Culloden Viaduct, Culloden, May 2017.

Girders

LNER A4 No. 60009 *Union of South Africa* at Montrose, May 2014.

Into the Storm

Virgin Trains Class 390 Pendolino threads the Lune Gorge, Tebay, August 2012.

Straw Bales

Virgin Trains Class 390 Pendolino at Bay Horse, July 2015.

Aqueduct

LMS Black 5 No. 44932 at Chirk, April 2014.

Winter Fog on the Canal

SR rebuilt West Country No. 34052 *Lord Dowding* (aka No. 34046 *Braunton*) runs along the Kennet & Avon Canal at Crofton, December 2016.

Bridges Old and New

Tyne and Wear Metro crosses the River Tyne with the King Edward VII Railway Bridge in the background, Newcastle upon Tyne, February 2007.

GWR King No. 6024 *King Edward I* at Kingswear, August 2011.

The Photographer

LNER K4 *The Great Marquess* run along the North Sea cliffs below Warsett Hill, March 2013.

Into the Sunset

LNER B12/3 No. 8572 (61572) with the Quad-Art coaches between Sheringham and Weybourne, North Norfolk Railway, November 2014.

Frosty Start

LMS Fairburn Tank No. 42073 departs Haverthwaite,
Lakeside & Haverthwaite Railway, November 2016.

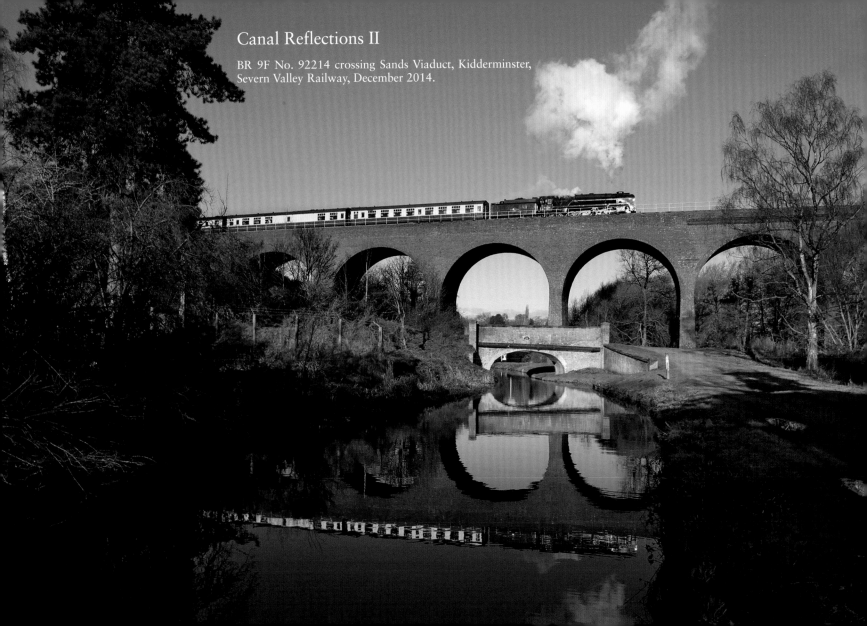

Canal Reflections II

BR 9F No. 92214 crossing Sands Viaduct, Kidderminster,
Severn Valley Railway, December 2014.

Bridges

LNER A4 No. 4464 (60019) *Bittern* crosses Dutton Viaduct, Dutton Lock, March 2014.

Edinburgh 200 Miles

LNER A4 No. 60007 *Sir Nigel Gresley* on the East Coast Main Line north of York, July 2008.

Industry

LMS Black 5 No. 45407 passes Tunstead Works (limestone), Great Rocks Dale, November 2008.

Pullman Train

SR Merchant Navy No. 35028 *Clan Line*,
Haslemere, March 2008.

M60

BR Standard 4 No. 76079 crosses the M60
motorway at Ashton Moss, December 2008.

The Thames–Clyde Express I

LMS Royal Scot No. 46115 *Scots Guardsman* at Moorcock, February 2008.

Skye Line

LMS Black 5 No. 45407 passes Loch a'Chiulinn, April 2008.

Far to the East

BR Britannia No. 70013 *Oliver Cromwell* at Oulton Broads, May 2009.

The Thames–Clyde Express II

LMS Royal Scot No. 46115 *Scots Guardsman* crosses Lunds Viaduct, Moorcock, August 2008.

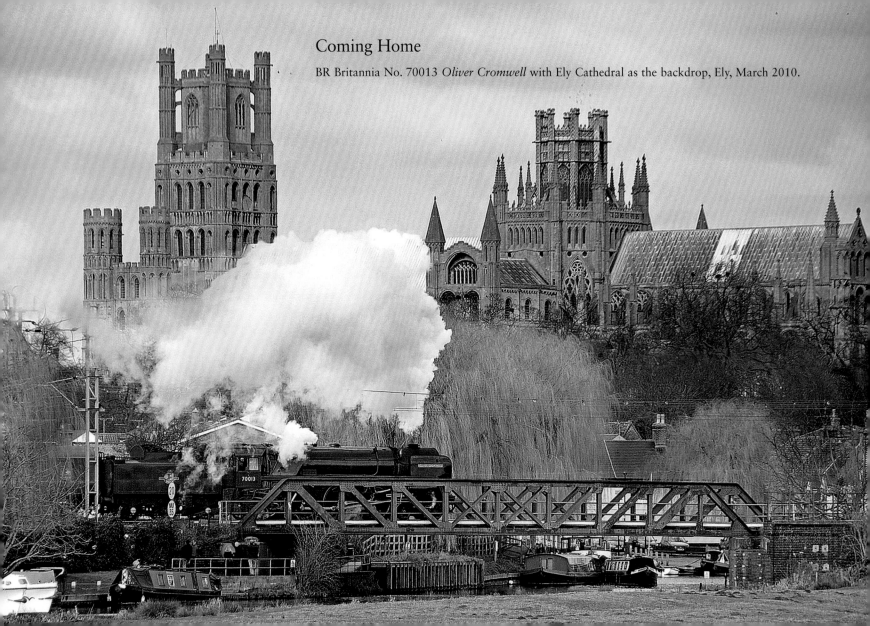

Coming Home

BR Britannia No. 70013 *Oliver Cromwell* with Ely Cathedral as the backdrop, Ely, March 2010.

Suspended II

LMS Royal Scot No. 46115 *Scots Guardsman* crosses the Forth Bridge, April 2012.

Blizzard

BR Britannia No. 70013 *Oliver Cromwell* at Kinchley Lane, Rotherley, Great Central Railway, February 2009.

Boundary

A1 Trust No. 60163 *Tornado* passes a cricket match at Pwll, July 2009.

Highest Station

Dent railway station on the Settle and Carlisle line, at 1,150 ft (350 m), is the highest operational main line station, December 2010.

Up from the Harbour

A British Railways Class 375 Electrostar passes along the main line while BR Britannia No. 70013 *Oliver Cromwell* climbs the harbour branch, Folkestone, March 2009.

Under Dark Skies

BR (WR) Pannier Tank No. 6412 near Staverton, South Devon Railway, February 2015.

Crabbing

BR Standard 4 No. 76079 leaves Barmouth while children fish for crabs, September 2009.

Ray of Light

Virgin Trains Class 390 Pendolino at Scout Green, January 2010.

Evening on the Tay

LMS Black 5 No. 45407 crossing the Tay Bridge between Dundee and Wormit, April 2009.

Steam Trail

LMS Black 5s Nos 44871 and 45407 alongside the Kennet & Avon Canal at Crofton, December 2014.

Crossing the Thames

A1 Trust No. 60163 *Tornado* on Grosvenor Bridge, aka Victoria Railway Bridge, August 2009.

Rolling Hills

Ex-Sierra Leone Railway No. 85 (WLR 14) approaches Llanfair Caereinion, Welshpool & Llanfair Light Railway, March 2008.

Highland River

LMS Black 5 No. 45407 crossing Gaur Viaduct, Rannoch, October 2014.

Eilean Na

LMS Black 5 No. 45305 passing Craig Highland Farm, Craig, April 2012.

Scottish Magic

LNER K1 No. 62005 crosses Glenfinnan Viaduct, Glenfinnan, October 2014.

Loch Reflections

LNER K4 No. 61994 *The Great Marquess* crosses
Loch Dubh, Polnish, October 2014.

Looking out to Barmouth Bay

LMS Black 5 No. 45407 crosses the Mawddach Estuary on Barmouth Bridge, Barmouth, August 2010.

West Highland Line

A ScotRail BR Class 156 approaches Rannoch railway station while LMS Black 5 No. 44871 waits to cross. Rannoch, October 2010.

Along the Loch

LNER K4 No. 61994 *The Great Marquess*, Loch Eilt, October 2014.

Backlit

LMS Black 5 No. 44871 and LMS Jubilee No. 5690 (45690) *Leander* climbing Shap at Scout Green, December 2010.

Snow on the Tyne

A Northern Rail BR Class 156 crosses the High Level Bridge, which carries both road and rail, Newcastle upon Tyne, January 2010.

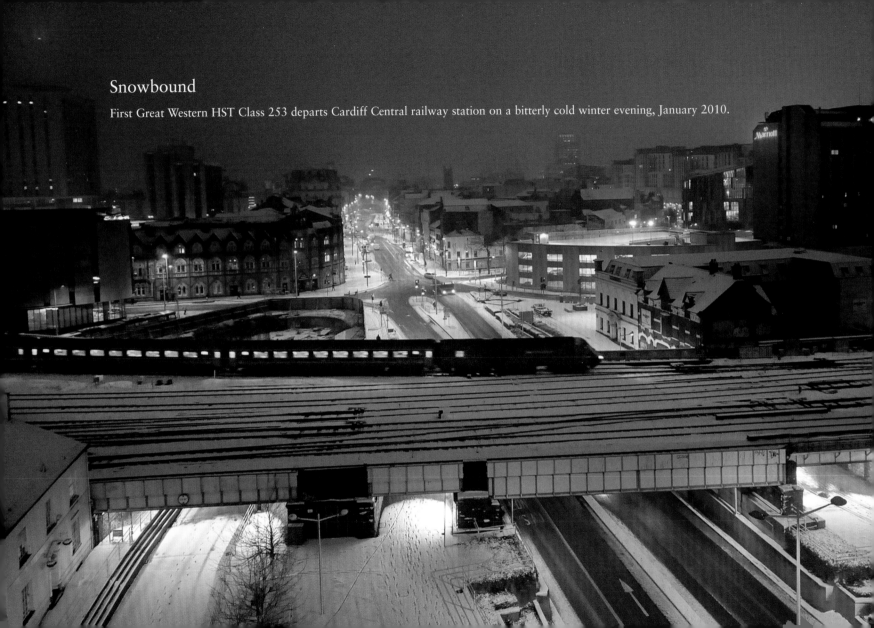

Snowbound

First Great Western HST Class 253 departs Cardiff Central railway station on a bitterly cold winter evening, January 2010.

Still waters

LMS Royal Scot No. 46115 *Scots Guardsman* crosses the River Lune at Lancaster, January 2010.

Steam Power

LNER A4 No. 4464 (60019) *Bittern* passes the cooling towers of the coal-fired Eggborough Power Station, Temple Hirst, April 2012.

Over the Summit

LMS Royal Scot No. 46115 *Scots Guardsman* breasts the summit and comes out into sunshine, Dromochter, April 2012.

Thunderstorm

BR Britannia No. 70000 *Britannia* waits to be coaled at Didcot Engine Shed, Didcot, August 2012.